POEMS AND RHYMES FROM NEAR AND FAR

Betty Gardner Harris

urbanpress

Poems and Rhymes From Near and Far
by Betty Gardner Harris
Copyright ©2019 Betty Gardner Harris

ISBN 978-1-63360-133-8
For Worldwide Distribution

Printed in the U.S.A.

Olive Trees by Vincent van Gogh, 1889
Cover art used with permission under the Creative Commons Zero (CC0) license

Urban Press
P.O. Box 8881
Pittsburgh, PA 15221-0881
412.646.2780

To God Be the Glory!

God the Father has set this appointed time, not to close a chapter of my life, but to open more for my future. My book of life has many chapters and now I take this opportunity to share a few chapters with you.

My name is Evangelist Missionary Betty Gardner. I was born May 29, 1947 to the union of Mr. Grant Lockett (Spad) and Mrs. Bernice Lockett. I am the second child born of their five children, and I have one sister and three brothers. I was born in Erie, Pennsylvania where I attended Burton Elementary School, but we soon relocated to Arkansas where I completed my education by graduating from Petit Jean Technical College.

Being a part of a dysfunctional family caused many changes in my life, especially the one where I married at fifteen years of age to escape all the abuse thrust upon me. With one daughter and two sons, I found myself a widow having to live on welfare. Today, I have eight grandchildren and ten great grandchildren. At this point, God placed His calling of a missionary on my life.

I always believed God had a plan for my life just as the Bible states: "I knew you even before you were conceived in your mother's womb" (see Jeremiah 1:5). For during the chapter of my life when I was raising my children, I found favor with God. He came to me in a vision letting me know that I would become a nurse. It came to pass, not an easy thing because when I first applied, I was not accepted. The school called me back, however, and because I was on welfare and a minority, I received free schooling to become a nurse. What God has for you no man can stop. It may be on delay but not denied.

The chapter of salvation came into existence when I was thirty years of age. I had another birthday to celebrate for I was given a new birth when I opened my heart to Jesus as He stood at the door of my heart and knocked. I opened the door and let him in and once the door was opened, salvation was accepted, and another chapter began.

My foreign mission work began at the age of forty-nine on my first trip to South Africa. What a spiritual uplifting time that was to be able to minister to God's children. God empowered me to go to Haiti, Dominican Republican, Zambia, Congo, and Ba' Congo. This journey opened another door for me in mission as I lived in South Africa for ten years in ten different provinces. My mission was working with children who had lost their parents to AIDS.

This book was written to awaken the conscience of those who live freely in a country with plenty where they are unaware of the needs of the people in developing countries. Yes, our fellow men, women, boys, and girls in that world have many needs. The poor we will always have, but if we find it in our power hands to help those in need, God will be pleased with us. What's more, the Bible tells us we could be entertaining angels and not be aware of it: "Every good thing bestowed and every perfect gift is from above coming down from the Father of lights, who cannot change" (James 1:17).

Betty Gardner Harris
Erie, PA
December 2019

Dedication

I dedicate this book to Mother Mary Beth Kennedy who inspired me to write it. Mother Kennedy is my mentor and I have walked a mile in her shoes. To be where she has gone has been a blessing to me and my ministry. I thank you for your love, caring spirit, and for showing me God's way to take care of His people and carry out the work of the Lord.

I also want to dedicate this book to my South African Pastor, Derrick Fynn, and his wife, Mrs. Mavis Fynn, of the Outreach Ministry, Sydenham, South Africa. God's blessings upon you all.

Bishop Charles E. Blake

He holds the position of Bishop International
and has a missions plan;
and with all the problems, he always remembers
our helpless fellow man.

Those who are needy, hungry, and sick,
no money in their hand;
our bishop is mindful of the Great Commission,
to do the best we can.

"Go into the world and carry this gospel"
is our Savior's command;
and while we are preaching the word of God,
they need natural food in their hand.

Please don't shut up your bowels of compassion,
but follow what Jesus planned;
there are so many who need our help,
as many as the grains of sand.

They need to know there is a better life
for them, after traveling through this land;
so join with me and pray for our Bishop,
as he leads this Christian band.

Mother Mary Beth Kennedy

This darling mother, an example is she,
a mentor, a confidante, a dear friend to me.

Her life as a missionary is second to none,
from Erie, PA, the best-kept secret to some.

Her knowledge for many years she has shared,
for the masses around the world she has cared.

She has played a great part in what I am now,
not only a missionary, but a poet somehow.

"Betty, you are gifted," she told me one day.
"Please put it on paper, you have so much to say."

I took her advice and the thoughts started to form,
and look at what's happened, the words are now poems.

God's gift to mankind, a dear lady is she;
I could never express what Mom means to me.

She never let her condition hold her back,
from the city to countries where there is much lack.

When able to walk, she carried full packs
of medicine and food strapped to her back.

At times she may suffer, but she is passing the test,
and all who know her feel we are so blessed.

For those who don't know her, you're missing a treat;
before she goes to heaven, our Mom you must meet.

Mom

M—is for magnificent, as everyone knows.
O—is for outstanding from her head to her toes.
T—is for teacher as her children grow strong.
H—is for husband, her star all the years long.
E—is for everything, that's all she could give.
R—is for righteous for as long as she lives.

Put them together and wherever she goes,
she serves as our mother who everyone knows.

To My Friend, Nickie

Dear friend,

When today my eyes came open,
I never ceased to pray.
I asked the Lord to guide me,
as I traveled through the day.

I know He hears my prayer, my friend,
that's why I prayed for you.

May He keep His loving arms around you,
while to missions I must go.

There's much work the Lord has assigned me,
exactly where I do not know.

So keep me in your prayers, my friend,
and often call my name.
And wherever I go, whether far or near,
I will always do the same.

Sister Betty's Thoughts

While flying on an airplane,
so many miles up high,
The days of my youth, so long ago,
came drifting to my mind.

I sat in a park on a bench one day
and looked up to the sky.
When a large plane went flying over,
I thought with a small sigh,
"Mr. Plane, Mr. Plane,
please stop and let me ride."

To remember life in my younger days
could easily make me cry.
More than fifty years have quietly passed,
I'm thinking now that I
have taken many, many trips
across God's great blue sky.

I'm called to do a job for Him,
much to my surprise,
that He would trust me, like He does,
to tend to children's cries.

Kai City is where I long to go,
along with other places;
it is a long and tedious journey there,
but I'll see so many faces.

Some people I have met before—
I wonder if they're there?
I often whisper to the Lord,
a quiet, simple prayer;
that He will please protect His own
as He has done for me,
before I traveled on my first trip
across His deep blue sea.

So if you long to work for Him,
just put it in His hands;
He knows the place you'll do your best
for Him and not for man.
And some day you'll grow old, my friend,
and time will take its toll;
then to heaven you will go
and rest your weary soul.

Heaven

Heaven is a lovely place,
the streets are paved with gold.
Oh, how I long to go there,
to rest my weary soul.

Don't get me wrong, my dearest one,
a hurry I am not;
but when my time is at an end,
and judgment is my lot,
I want to live in heaven,
no visiting there for me.
It will be my final resting place,
my Savior's face I'll see.

I'll sit around the throne of God
and praise Him day and night.
And all the saints who've gone before,
will worship in His sight.

He gave His life for you and me,
in pain and suffering;
the scars He bore on Calvary's cross
were not a pleasant thing,

But now He's back in heaven
with His Father patiently,
preparing a place that's just
for us to live continually.

Oh yes, my friend, you have a place,
prepared for you there, too.
So come along, prepare yourself,
your mansion is brand new.

We Owe Him

All to Jesus, do we sing.

All to Him let praises ring.

Shouts of triumph to our King.

Hail the power of Jesus' name.

All to Jesus, do we sing.

Old Story

There is an old, old story,
and no, there's nothing new,
of Jesus up in glory and how
He died for me and you.

The story, you see,
is written in the oldest book that's known.
It tells of wonderous works of God
who's sitting on His throne.

Now all you need is to have faith
the size of a mustard seed,
and close your eyes in silent prayer
and tell Him what you need.

Believe our God is listening
and this I feel is true—
no matter the request or problem,
He knows what's best for you.

After you pray, say, "Thank You, Lord,
my need has been supplied."
I myself have tried Him;
I've never been denied.

Trees

What is majestic
and sways in the wind;
large in its numbers,
can dance with its kin?

Seasons it changes,
in Fall loses leaves?
To answer the question,
I'm thinking of trees.

They come in all sizes,
from sprigs to great oaks;
in summer, they shade us,
from youth to old folk.

Quite large they can grow,
some mammoth, some small;
some used for our shelter,
some used not at all.

So please don't abuse them,
we need them, you know;
and it takes many years
for a live tree to grow.

The Cross

Let the bells sweetly ring and choirs softly sing.
The worst is now over, we hail our great King.
One day He was greeted with triumphal cries,
yet only one week later, our Savior He dies.

Those who loved Him, all grieved and moaned.
Those who hated, they spit and they stoned.
Our Lord and Savior, on a tree He died,
so all our needs could be richly supplied.

All hail the power of Jesus' name;
He did not come for gain or fame.
But just for us, our Savior came;
endured the cross but rose again.

Believe

Some don't believe there is a God;
they don't believe they can be lost.

Some think they die and that is all;
no burning hell for them wherein they fall.

But listen, my friend, you've got it all wrong,
for our God is sitting upon His throne.

He's gone ahead just to prepare,
a place for us to live up there.

Now I'm not sure where heaven is;
some say on earth, some in the air.

But it's all right, for this I know,
wherever He is, I want to go.

Sunday School

Sunday School has started,
so hurry, we are late.
We never want to miss it;
the teaching is so great.

We'll learn about the Golden Rule,
the Bible we are taught.
It tells about the saints of old
and the battles they have fought.

But now those saints are resting;
they all have said goodbye.
We may not be as great as they,
but, Lord knows, we will try.

Love

I love you, my darling, and trust you, I do.
I determine to have no other but you.
So please, my dear sweetheart, do love me the same.
You gave me your body; you gave me your name.

I bore you your children, which I was happy to do.
Whatever makes you happy, I'll always be true.
No one comes before you, you have not a clue,
I love you, my darling, I love you, I do.

I promised in marriage till death us do part.
I said those words, dearest, they came from my heart.
So if ever in doubt, my dear loved one, just ask,
and I'll repeat the same vows, I have said in the past

Seasons

It's getting chilly, the season is changing.
Winter is on the way, it's also been raining,

And sometime dreary, but really a beautiful day.
We must admit, we have no control over the weather.

So what can we do but bundle up warmly,
and enjoy it, me and you?

Alpha and Omega

He's Alpha and Omega,
the beginning and the end.
He's always here to comfort
and to love us, my friend.

So if you will believe,
and have faith in our God today,
He'll be right there whenever you need Him—
just never cease to pray.

He will come to your rescue;
He is with you at all times.
What a great and mighty God we have,
I'm glad He is mine.

Bugs

There was a mud hole in the middle of a swamp where many bugs lived. As they grew and became strong, they would climb up on a lily pad. The climb was very high and so when the bugs arrived at the top, they lay in the sun to rest. After waking they would stretch themselves and find that they had wings and as the mud would crack and fall off, the wings would come out. And as the wings moved, to the bugs' surprise, they could fly and so they flew all around and never returned.

One day, one of the smaller bugs said, "When I am big, I'm going to climb up the lily pad and see what is going on. I wonder why everyone goes up and never returns? Then I'll come back and tell you all what is happening."

So the day came when the bug was old enough to climb up the lily pad. The trip up was very tiring so when he reached the top, he laid down to rest. The sun was shining and he had a good sleep. When he awoke, he began to stretch himself, only to discover the mud cracked and the bug had wings under the mud. As he began to move around, he found that he too could fly. Up and down, up and down, the little bug flew.

He was so excited that he flew over to the place where he had made the long journey up the stem of the lily pad, and remembered what he had said to those he left behind about coming back to let them know what happened to the others who had gone on before him. He looked at the mud hole and then decided, "No, I won't go back, I will let them come up and see for themselves."

I believe this may be the story of those who have made the journey to heaven. It is so lovely there that they refuse to return and share what it's like. I can hear them saying, "No, I won't go back. I think I'll just let them come and see for themselves."

Go.....................d

"Go into the world and preach the Word,
for there are many people who still have not heard.
the free, unadulterated Scripture," He said.
Jesus won't come back 'til His holy Word is spread.

Our Lord wants all mankind to be fed,
and how can they be fed if they are not led?
Therefore, our mission is not nearly through;
missionaries, there's still so much work to do.

You say of yourself that you have been called.
So again I say, no, I plead with you all.
Get up, get busy, there is much work to do;
our Lord is with us, He will see us through.

Beif and Chris

On the day you both met
and looked in each other's eyes;
you thought to yourselves,
"We're in love," and you smiled.

You knew right that minute together you'd be—
not just a short while, but for eternity.

The Bible says love hides a multitude of faults,
so keep the love sweetened with sugar not salt.

So come on, you guys, you've had a great start.
I truly love you; you're both in my heart.

Love,

Mom

Walk in the Light

Walk in the light, so bright and so fair,
knowing that God is joining you there.

Find comfort in Him, His love is so true;
whatever you need, He'll give it to you.

So if in a valley or on a mountain oh so high,
just call when you need Him, He'll answer your cry.

Christmas

It soon will be Christmas, a beautiful sight;
the neighborhood lit with the twinkling of light.

The Christ-child so happy in His cradle He lay;
born in a manger, one fine Christmas day.

The people are singing carols in the street,
smiling and waving at whoever they meet.

Oh, come and adore Him, this sweet little Lamb,
who later announces, He's the great I am.

Give Love Away

Love is not love until given away;
God has blessed you to find love to stay.

No love is sweeter than when your soulmate you find;
so now he is yours and he says, "You're mine."

You searched the world over and now it is true,
my darling soulmate, I finally found you.

We'll stay together till the end of all time;
so glad I found you, so glad you are mine.

We promise to honor and respect in all ways;
this vow we will keep for the rest of our days.

No one before you, not ever again;
from now and forever, we are best of friends.

Chimes

The wind blows the chimes, first this way and that.

We can never be sure of just where they're at.

It's Jesus who has control o'er the wind.

He knows where it goes and where it has been.

Valentine

Please be mine and always stay close

beside me, my love, I do pray.

My heart is happy to be where you are,

and there's where I long to stay.

Lobola

You paid the lobola of 21 cows;
was it worth the wait?
It took a long time to save up the money—
you could not get in the gate.

You know how protective my mama and aunties are,
my darling, 'tis true.
Today we saw each other at church,
and you really did look quite blue.

I'll make you happy, my darling, I promise,
for you have worked so hard.
We'll jump the broom and be in a hurry,
and then leave them in the yard.

They'll be so busy eating the food
provided by you and I.
We'll make our escape, and they won't find us—
not even if they try,

Married

Today we have married, my dearest best friend,
we've been in love for a very long time.

Love is not all we will share
but whatever is yours is mine.
We have little habits that we have been hiding,
oh dear, why wasn't I told?

For better or worse, is what we agreed;
the vows were from days of old.

We should have written our own vows,
this I know is true;
but now we said yes to the traditional setting,
we must be happy, I and you.

To Mission

On a mission journey again I go,
the work has been assigned;
to many places in deepest Africa,
I'll see people of all kinds.

Some wear clothes and some do not;
it's part of their culture, you see.
Some of them shocked when I go there;
they have never seen a black missionary.

They sing and dance when I enter the camp;
The big iron pots cooking the beans and the samp.

They killed a cow to celebrate those who came.
They cooked the cow, yes, cooked the whole thing,
and we ate everything but its name.

The chickens in the pen are nice and plump,
a few will lose their life.

Someone wring the chickens' necks;
then someone bring the knife.

It may sound awful to kill the meat,
but where else would we get something to eat?

Daddy

He's there when I need him, oh so much.
He gives me my bath with his gentle touch.

He holds me and loves me whenever I sleep.
He teaches me to pray my soul to keep.

And if I fall down, he picks me up.
He lets me drink tea from his big cup.

Sometime when he's gone, I miss him so.
I want to go find him, my mummy says no.

She'll never understand the love we share.
I know if no one else, my Daddy does care.

He works very hard to take care of us.
We don't have to worry—in Daddy we trust.

And when I am big and Daddy is old,
I'll take care of him; he'll never be cold.

I'll tuck him in as he has done me.
Daddy don't worry, just wait and you'll see.

Daddy Went Away

"Please don't leave us, please don't go."
I heard a small voice as Dad closed the door.
"Daddy doesn't live here anymore;
he left us to travel to a distant shore,"

It's very hard for us to understand
why dying is part of God's holy plan.
We loved our dad, yes, we loved him so—
some day we will know why he had to go.

Till then my sister and I will take care of each other,
and we thank the Lord that we still have our mother.

South Africa

Birds are singing, sun is shining,
and children are having fun.
The life they live is normal to them,
they don't have a care, no not one.

We are blessed in the U.S.,
so many miles away.
I cannot help but envy them though
as I watch them romp and play.

They laugh and run and don't complain
of the shortages they meet,
even if sometimes it happens,
they don't have food to eat.

But those of us from the U.S.
who have visited their land, our hearts
are sad for our sisters and brothers,
for they are our fellow man.

So the very next time I feel to complain
of the food I have to eat,
Lord, help me remember,
my friends and kin in Africa without meat.

To visit those in Africa
who love you so much,
with loving eyes and great big smiles
and child-like tender touch.

Yes, we are so blessed in the USA
but forget our fellow man.
God, please won't You forgive,
and help us to understand.

We have so much that we could share;
there are many of us who can.
Please help us to remember,
dear Lord, it's all part of Your plan.

One day we will come to meet You
and this I feel is true.
You'll ask the question to all of us,
"Tell me, what did you do?"

You heard the missions beg for help,
to tend to the needy cry.
My friend, you will have no excuse—
and by the way, neither will I.

So next time that the basket is passed,
and an offering you will give.
Please remember in your heart,
those who need help to live.

And when you stand before the throne,
you'll hear our Savior say,
"Come in, my dear, you have done your part;
you are welcome here to stay."

Big Pig

I gave them money to buy a pig.
They brought it home today with legs bound tight
with nice strong rope, so not to get away.

The children were so excited,
they all clapped hands and said,
"Oh, thank You, Lord, for we'll have
meat before we go to bed.
Yes, thank You, Lord, for we'll have
meat before we go to bed."

"We'll see pork chops, loins, and ribs,
all beautiful and pink;
they'll be cut up and washed so nice and clean,
in the makeshift African sink."

"Now friends, we want to welcome you,
please come and share our dish.
For those of you who don't eat pork,
we'll serve you up some fish."

Good Pig

They are waiting for the pig to cook
in a large pot outside.
They say they saved some of it
so we could have a braai.

It doesn't matter how you cook it,
bake, boil, or braai.
The pig has made a sacrifice,
so that we could stay alive.

A Song

There's a song in my heart,
I believe this is true;
the music only starts
when I'm thinking of you.

I hum a happy, joyful tune,
you're soon to come home;
I can hardly wait my love,
till we will be alone.

So we get all the dishes washed,
and tuck the kids in bed;
and don't forget to read to them—
that's what the Scripture said.

And by the time all is done
and all the lights turned down,
you're snoring love and I am, too—
we'll make another round.

Home Again, Home Again, Jiggity Jig

I watched them kill a pig today
and much to my surprise,
they set the pig on fire
right before my eyes.

They hit him in the head, quite hard,
until he did expire;
then covered him with much-dried leaves,
and then they lit the fire.

I am told we will have lots of meat
to feed the people Sunday;
so get up early and come to church
and we'll all enjoy a fun day.

Before we eat, we'll thank the Lord,
for all that He has done;
for all He has provided,
we'll thank Him everyone.

And when it's time to go to bed,
I'll thank the Lord again,
for how He has provided food
for me and all my friends.

Cessareana

My sister, Rena, works so hard
to cook, to wash and clean;
I feel she is so special,
the best sister I've ever seen.

We heard the news our sis was ill,
and I said, "Mother please,
can you help me go to her
so with my own eyes I can see?"

So here I am at sister's house;
my desire has been fulfilled.
I can see sister for myself;
thank God my sister's healed.

Jesus Is Born

"We have no room in the inn,"
they heard the keeper say.
"There is only the stable in the back,
with animals and hay."

With great concern, Joseph turned,
looked at Mary and said,
"The town is filled, there's no more room.
There's only straw for the babe to lay."

So the baby Christ-child, our dear Lord,
in a humble setting came;
a gift from our Father in heaven,
Jesus is His name.

He came to save mankind from sin,
that was His Father's plan;
If they had known who was to come,
they would have given a helping hand.

"I need You to go down, my Son;
You're the only one who can,
for the man I created for My use
now needs a helping hand."

Now He is here; don't turn your back,
because if you do, you'll fail.
This is the truth, my dear friend,
this is no fairy tale.

Africa

There is much work in Africa;
I know God has a plan.
We must stay busy, all of us,
to help our fellow man.

Some say it's hard to do this work,
but they don't understand.
We give our all for Jesus
and do the best we can.

Then when our time is over,
and we go back to the dust,
our souls will then go back to God—
our God in whom we trust.

We Owe Him

All to Jesus do we sing.

All to Him let praises ring.

Shouts of triumph, to our King.

Hail the power of His name.

Big Book

When the book is opened and our names are called
and all the deeds accomplished.
Whether big or small, all have been recorded
in the big book opened wide.

At the great white throne of God,
with Jesus by His side,
we'll stand before our Savior—
there will be no place to hide.
We want to go to heaven, forever to reside.

Now if you did not live for Him,
then hell will be your place.
There is no use to plead with Him,
when you finally see His face.

He has sent you all the warnings
in the word of God.
So please, my friend, don't go to hell—
forever is a long, long time.

Cousin Bay

I really thank God for my cousin Bay;
it is a joy to see her from day to day.

A lovely smile, sharp as a tack;
she prays for me, always has my back.

A wonderful cook, so neat and clean;
bakes the best pound cake you've ever seen.

God, please bless my cousin and do let her stay;
her name is Catherine, but we call her Bay.

Children

To watch the children training
as they learn things to do,
they are washing clothes on their hands—
for me this is brand new.

Oh, thank You, Lord, for washing machines,
we just put in the plugs.
But they carry water on their heads in five-gallon jugs.

To teach them they start out early,
when first they learn to walk.
Then they put something on their head
as first they learn to talk.

Before long they are trained to work,
complaining they don't do.
So raise your children just like them,
you'll hear less complaining, too.

The Mamas

The older mamas came early,
they're sitting in the yard;
they asked for money to buy food,
the life for them is hard.

They killed a pig yesterday;
he is cooking in a pot, so
leave before the pig is done—
no darling, they will not.

Cassava Leaves

I watched them pound cassava leaves,
in a great big wooden bowl.
They beat them over and over
with a long thick wooden pole.

Then they prepared to cook the leaves
in a great big iron pot.
They poured oil in over the fire
until it was very hot.

The food will soon be ready
for a wonderful Sunday lunch.
And all our friends, both far and near,
will enjoy it all so much.

We Smell Food

Pots are boiling in the yard,
the people passing by,
are smelling something cooking good
and thinking, "Me, oh my!"

They stop out on the road to see,
what here is going on;
and then they hear the ladies
start to sing a lovely song.

They are singing in their language,
I think I know the tune.
I hum along in my own tongue;
I want to learn their language soon.

Africa Again

Over the deep wide ocean,
under the sunny sky,
the Lord has smiled on my again—
in Africa am I.

To tell the Bible story of Jesus
and His love;
He's waiting there in glory,
our home prepared above.

So don't you want to meet Him,
in heaven there to stay?
Well, you better get ready, you never know.
He may call you home today.

Frank's Town

A beautiful girl is Lucy; at times she looks so sad.
The life she has lived these 16 years
has really not been so bad.
She lives with Connie and Frank;
they have loved her like their own.

They rescued her from a very bad fate,
and gave her a lovely home.
I know some day they will get old,
and never have to plead,
from anyone, not far or near;
they will never have a need.

Because of how they took in Lucy,
although she is not their seed.
"Dear Lord, bless Frank and Connie Fynn,
they took in many to feed."

Someday the book will open,
the angel will call their names.
They'll stand before our loving God;
we'll all have to do the same.

The deeds that we accomplish,
will all be written down;
but Connie and Frank will be rewarded
for what they did in Frank's Town.

Drums

I listened to the drums last night
as I tried to sleep;

I tried everything last night,
including counting sheep.

But after trying oh so long,
I finally gave up and said,

"Lord, why don't You make them sleepy,
so they will go to bed?"

No Fanta, No Coke

"Papa, we have a feast today, and I can see no Coke."
Papa said, "Sorry, my son,
Coke costs money and this is not a joke."
"But, Papa, we must pray for God to give us and He
will."
Papa said, "Okay, my son, we will pray, now you be
still."

Death

Many people scream and cry,
a loved one has just passed.
Though others try to comfort them
and say that life can't last.

We all must leave this place,
we must go, I and you.
None of us came here to stay,
we all must bid adieu.

So we must then prepare ourselves,
for we will be leaving, too.
Our Jesus has a home for us;
in heaven it's brand new.

Heaven

Over in that great beyond,
our Lord for us awaits.
He's standing there to open wide,
those wondrous pearly gates.

The streets are paved with gold,
what the Bible says is true.
I'm making ready to go there
and I know that you are, too.

Two Women One Man

Yesterday I was told two wives to just one man.
I need the Lord to help me; I just don't understand.

How a man can feed two wives,
with children from the two?
He leaves some of them hungry;
husband, shame on you!

Cessareana

They called my sister Reana in,
the doctor finally came;
how I was oh so happy,
when they called my sister's name.

Big sister there went with her,
while pastor moved the car;
I am praying now that all is well,
my sister lives so far.

America is a long way off;
I wish it was not true;
dear sister, I do wish,
I could live closer to you.

Lover

Think how lonely you would be,
if God had not blessed you to find me.

I'm your good thing the Bible says,
and so, I'm the answer to your prayers.

The love we have God gave to us;
He's our head, so in Him we trust.

You are the star on our family tree;
promise to stay together for eternity.

And should the Lord call you home,
and in this world, we no more roam.

Just remember, like from the start,
you will always remain here in my heart.

Easter Sunday

'Twas on a hill my Savior died,
on that same place was crucified.
He did no wrong for me He died;
I could not pay, not if I tried.

A life of sin my Lord forgave;
He rescued me and now I'm saved.
From all the filth born into man,
He cleaned me up, that was His plan.

Shaped and molded me in His hand;
Oh, what a friend we have in Him.
Who gave His life out on the limb
of a tree, just think, His Father created.
"Forgive them, Father," is what He stated.

"They have no idea, no not a clue.
If I called for help, what You would do?
I have all power in my hands."

"So help them Father, to understand
that soon one day, I will return
to give them pay they did not earn."

Forgive

It doesn't matter what they have done;
you must forgive them, every one.

Jesus forgave when nailed to the cross;
if He had not, then our souls would be lost.

He said, "Do unto others as you would have done;
love all your enemies, yes every one."

Then when it's all over and you draw your last breath,
when your eyes will close, you will surrender to death.
You won't have to worry, to heaven you'll go.

The problem, my friend, is when we don't know.
So always keep forgiveness there in your heart,
and when life is over, you have done your part.

Easter Sunday

I woke up early this morning, it's Resurrection Day.
Our Jesus Christ has promised
that He would return today.
The women went to the tomb, failed to find Him there.

Oh, how they wept and mourned
when they found the tomb was bare.
They saw two angels standing by
and began to enquire of them.

"Please tell us where they took our Lord;
we've come to tend to Him."
Their hearts were broken when they saw
the napkin on the stone it lay.

But our Lord was not there,
and they were worried that someone stole His body
away.
So the angels said, "Do not worry. Our Lord is alive
He has risen just like He said.
He kept His promise; He is not dead."

Our Lord is alive.

Travel

Our God is here, our God is there,
our God is everywhere.

No need to fret, no need to worry,
He loves us and He cares.

So give your problems all to Him,
He will your burdens share.

It doesn't matter big or small,
our God is there to carry them all.

Wide awake or in a deep sleep,
our God is there, our souls to keep.

Our God is everywhere.

Leaves

Swirling and blowing, dancing with the wind,
beautiful colors, the oranges and greens—
the most interesting shades you have ever seen.

Our God created all trees strong or lean;
He is the most talented artist, can design any scene.

Can you imagine just how it would be
if our God had created leaves without trees?

Roots of the trees all travel to find,
water for nourishment, roots of all kind.

The more they are nourished, the larger they grow;
how far they may travel, only God really knows.

Under the grounds, they travel so far.
If you find them all tangled, hard to know whose they are.

The tree is so special, provides many needs,
from men building houses to nice polished skis.

So be careful to put all your campfires out,
so trees can continue to grow big and stout.

A Home

We have a home in glory, our Lord went to prepare;
He promised He would have a place
for me when I get there.

It may be in the morning, could be night or noon;
I don't need to worry, whether it's late or soon.

Oh, I want to see Him, with Him be there to reign.
There will be no sorrow and there will be no pain.

When the gates swing open and I go inside,
I want to live with Him, forever to reside.

Love

For the rest of our lives we promise to love;
we want to be close as a hand in a glove.
We found our true soulmate, though it did take time;
now I am yours and I'm glad you are mine.

We want to grow old together and
see the door close behind the last baby.
They will go to college or wherever they choose,
after eighteen we have paid our dues.

But up until then, we are happy to be,
me loving you and you loving me.
Love is an action word, it's easy to do;
especially, my darling, when the love is so true.

We will stick to each other like good super glue,
and if we get angry, we may throw a shoe.
But we promise from now on to love faithfully,
to share all we have, my dear, you and me.

Paul

We prayed for Paul a very long time;
there was a day when his light did shine,
But somehow got wounded along the way;
on Sunday morning at home he would stay.

Now, I don't know how Paul would feel,
for he knew God was all so real.
He would work hard from Monday on,
but on Sunday morning, Paul had no song.

Just had a problem going to church;
It was his to sort out—he had to search.
He was unhappy that we could see,
"But why, oh Lord, how can it be?"

"I knew my friend, Paul, truly loved Thee;
he just could not seem to break free,
Of this thing that had him bound,
this thing that seemed so profound."

"Keep on praying" is what I would say;
"I believe he will preach someday."
Paul loves God oh so much,
and I know God someday will touch.

He'll be the best, just wait and see,
the husband for Ruth and a friend to me.
Well, the day has finally come,
our Paul is shining for everyone.

His light is bright and we now can see
what a great man he can truly be,
an example to everyone, he is now free.
He's a great husband to Ruth,
and a great friend to me.

Meka Jean

M – Is for Marvelous, this sweet little girl.
E – Is for Everything to Nickie and Earl.
K – Is for Kindness, she's such a sweet pearl.
A – Is for All, she's loved by the world.
J – Is for Jesus, heaven's babe sent.
E – Is for Envied at each family event.
A – Is for Apple of her papa's eye.
N – Is for Nonsense, she has never been shy.

We are all blessed God gave us this child;
her heart is so soft, is not easily riled.
Just like a baby so helpless and mild—
big shiny eyes, and a beautiful smile.

We all must be careful to help her to grow;
how long she'll be with us, we truly don't know.
But love her we will with all of our hearts;
we will teach her and train her till death we do part.

And when it shall happen to heaven we go, we'd
have trained her 'bout Jesus—His word we will sow.
She will know how He loves her and go on to be,
the best sanctified lady anybody will see.

They Branded Me

This spirit within that has me bound,
the strongest spirit that can be found.

It started to grow when I was young;
I had no protection from anyone.

And now this spirit which tries to destroy,
not just the mature, but the little boys.

I want deliverance, Lord, help me, please,
to rid my body of this disease,
that has me twisted in its clutch.
When I must endure that dreaded touch,
of the hand that defiles me so much.

I know it's wrong; it is not your plan, but God,
the people really don't understand
what this spirit has done to man.

Love

Allow him to love you, don't turn him away,
because if you do, you'll be sorry someday.

He paid for your body till death you do part;
you owe him your everything, including your heart.

You told him you loved him right from the start;
so come on, my sister, now you do your part.

It's time to get busy, it's time to come clean;
we know you are pregnant, but don't treat him so
mean.

He told you he's sorry, he repented and all;
he loves you, my sister, please heed to his call.

The Shelter

They come early to the door;
if they could, would come at four.

So much danger on the street,
hard to find a place to sleep.

Coffee pot plugged in at six,
male and female, they are mixed.

Made mistakes along the way,
most times sorry that they strayed.

From their teachings early on,
they received when they were young.

Well, thank God for a place to go,
out of the cold, the rain, and snow.

Won't You touch the weary hearts
that no matter where they are,
and no matter what they do,
they will come to depend on You.

For the day soon will surely come,
when we will meet You everyone.

Down here, we may not have a place,
but up in heaven, there is a space.

What a day that will be,
when Your precious face we see.

When we hear You as You say,
"You are welcome here to stay."

Believe It or Not

Some say He's coming, some say He's not;
they say there is no hell, and some say it's hot.
The Bible confirms it in Luke twenty-two;
it tells us what Jesus was about to do.

"This is my blood given for you,"
He told His disciples, "and my body eat, too.

The time is coming, I'll be betrayed."
When the time came His life he laid
down for all people, not just for a few.
He went to the cross for me and for you.

Someday He's coming, so whatever you do,
please get ready. Irwin, I am talking to you.

Cleve and Shelly Ann

We have seen many faces, down through the years,
lost many loved ones, shed many tears.
All through high school, we never had a fear;
we knew we would find each other, whether far or
near.

Didn't have to worry, didn't have to care;
we took our time to live our lives like the Bible said.
Obedient to our parents, always said our prayers.
They told us, "If you keep yourself,
God will give you what is fair."

A mate that's fashioned just for me
was on the Master's wheel;
He knew who we were looking for;
He knows just how you feel.
My darling, you are all I need,
my needs you do fulfill;
we don't have to worry, our lives
we will always share.

We will work hard, have plenty of babies,
and then someday we will see,
how living a clean and sanctified life,
has paid off for you and me.

Good Night

Sorry I had to leave you, I was not with you very long,
It was time to join the choir,
and they were rehearsing a new song.
No one else knew the verses, so I was called to lead;
you know how I always liked to help out,
whenever there was a need.

My time was well spent,
I had lots of family and friends,
and some of you I didn't get close to,
before my time was at an end.
It's really beautiful here, though,
the kind of place you'd like to live.

If I had more time, more service I would have given;
but all of you here tonight, I have a message just for you.
Please get ready now, as death is coming for you, too.
Don't continue to take chances, don't you wait too late;
the Lord is here waiting, He's standing at the gate.
My suffering is over, my flesh could take no more;
but I found that it was worth it, where I am now.

You see I am in a new body now—no pain, no agony.
I hope you will get ready, for our Savior's face to see.

It's true He has a big book, and everything we do,
is written in that book, believe me, this is true.

The life you live on earth is such a special gift;
be careful how you use it—don't stand out on a cliff.
Because when your life is over,
and you stand before God's throne,
you'll be standing there all by yourself—
we all must stand alone.

Well, now you have the message,
I hope you heed the call.
It's time to say goodnight, you guys,
please know I love you all.

Connie Fynn

Oh, what a homemaker,
she won't even use a maid;
takes care of Frank's Town,
for very little pay.

A wonderful aunty second to none,
no one can compare, nobody not one.
She's Cody's mama when he's in distress;
he screams for her loudly and clings to her dress.

"Oh, Mama, I love you," I heard Cody say,
"Please pick me up from the table,
for I want to go and play."

Flowers

Flowers of all kinds, created by God,
all sizes, all colors, some shaped very odd.

Depends on the climate, may bloom all year round;
they grow, oh so beautiful, yet don't make a sound.

Only God our Creator can make such as these;
some ever so big, they grow tall like trees.

Some are nourished by pollen from bees;
sometimes they grow wild so everyone sees.

If I want to name them, I'm sure I don't know.
So watch how we treat them, as we watch them grow—
for we love seeing flowers wherever we go.

Home for Some

The night is quiet and all is still,
baby has gone to sleep.
I lay done after saying my prayers,
Father, my soul to keep.

We are so blessed in this lovely place,
a night place to lay our head.
There are many with no place to rest,
their children have not even been fed.

Thinking of those who lay under the stars,
with cardboard for a bed.
My heart is sore when they cross my mind,
for I see them in a cardboard shed.

The stores are closed, shopkeepers gone,
home to their comfortable beds.
But these, the homeless,
I now can see, have only the night to dread.

Some women dress like men,
with caps pulled down o'er their faces.
It's because if they don't,
they will be in dangerous places.

God help the poor who have not what we do,
and cannot share a space.
Forgive us, Lord, who share not compassion,
no, we won't share a trace.

Noxolo

With a beautiful child, just six years old,
a lady came to see me.
She was very heart sore.
"Please Sister Betty, I do implore,
I pray that you can help me."

I went over to visit my neighbor today,
she lay helpless on a rug made of straw.
I was so sad when I looked and I saw,
a mother suffering and dying with AIDS.

She was being looked after by her six-year-old babe;
the child had cooked rice, doing the best that she could,
in a big iron pot with a few scraps of wood.

She said, "Sister Betty, can you help me, please?
I myself suffer from this awful disease."

I asked, "Can you bring the poor lady to me?"

She said, "I don't think so, she is so weak, as you see.
And I don't have money and they do live quite far.
Please, can you help me to bring them by car?"
I gave her money, just trusting that she
would keep her word and bring the people to me.

83

The very next day, to my utmost surprise,
the lady was standing before my eyes
with this darling little girl, so very small.

I picked up the phone and made a call.
"God bless you, Dr. Albu," for he quickly said,
"Yes, you may take the mom and give her a bed."

In the infirmary that day we went;
thank God for the neighbor, she was heaven sent.
I spoke to the mom and asked her if she was saved.
She said no, I told her about heaven, and she wanted to go.

"Will you take care of my baby when I go home?
I don't want to leave her here all alone."
I said, "Rest in the Lord, leave her to me.
The Lord will provide, we just thank Him you're free."

Two days later the mom went to sleep;
the Lord has provided for the child we keep.
She is now a teenager, a sweet, loving child.
Thank God for doctors and for life.

Welcome

When the gates swing open and I go inside,
I will reign with Jesus, forever to reside.

I'll see our God in heaven sitting on His throne, saying,
"Your work is done, weary pilgrim, welcome home."

Someday, Someday

Someday the Lord will call our name
when our work is done.
We will have no more pain,
or sorrows—no not one.

We will see our loved ones who have gone before;
most of all, we'll see our Lord standing at door.
He will say, "You did your best," for He knows I tried;
many times I was not sure—He saw me when I cried.

He knows I fed the hungry, that's what I was to do;
and sometimes, I was to give them shelter—
He knows I did that, too.

The Camps

When we visit squatter camps and we see the poor,
some don't have much food to eat
while we have food and more.

I know that God is watching to see what we will do,
for by His grace there goes I,
and it could have been you, too.

I thank God every day because I gave all I could give.
I feel this is my mission here;
He gave me this place to live.

The Lord wants us to do our best,
we must help the poor;
we must lead them all to Him,
to reign forevermore.

Remember, He did not give His life
just for you and your four;
He gave His life for all of us,
He is standing at the door.

With arms wide open to welcome
all His children to a home.

He has prepared for us to live—
never more to roam.

Oh, I want to see Him and look Him in His face,
there to sing forever of God's amazing grace.

Newlands East

Today we went to Newlands East to visit some saints
in the midst of a church.
If you are looking for a place of worship,
now you can end your search.

The pastor is great, the praise team is fine,
the Word of God was preached.
I was so glad they had loudspeakers
so Newlands East could be reached.

So many came for the altar call,
we had to move the chairs.
Many gave their hearts to God;
I may have seen you there.

Some who came cried out to God
with tears in all their eyes.
They went back home feeling new;
I know because so did I.
Just think how wonderful it will be
when we are caught up in the sky.

We're going to a place to live
where no one will ever die.

To go to that place you must be saved,
otherwise don't even try.
Just give your heart to God
and go to your mansion up on high.

Trees in the Wind

The wind is blowing, the trees are bending—
oh, what a beautiful sight.
And in the sunshine can look so lovely,
but at nighttime can give you a fright.

Have you ever walked in the forest at nighttime
among the great big oaks?
It can be scary walking alone;
I tell you this is no joke.

When I was young, I got lost in the woods;
I ran away from home.
I felt so unloved and also unwanted
from my head down to my toes.

But I'm grateful to God
for how He protected and saved me from my sins;
He let me know I was forgiven—
He placed His love deep within.

Now with no problem
I can go walking in daytime or at night.
Study the bushes and trees as they grow
and love them with all of my might.

Pickering Street

So many people we ran out of seats,
I saw them gather at Pickering Street.

Most of them homeless, no shoes on their feet,
and some with no food to eat.

Some of them sick with AIDS on the rise,
no matter the color, no matter the size.

If God doesn't help them, they all will be lost;
we must introduce Him, no matter the cost.

Please, God, won't You strengthen
the leaders You have placed,
to teach Your dear children,
so they will see Your face.

All will go to heaven,
but some will not stay;
but we all want to stay there—
oh please help us, I pray.

Pastor and Mrs. Fynn

They have been together a very long time,
and sometime the way was not so fine.

Derrick and Mavis, one of a kind;
pastor could never get Mavis off his mind.
God called them to minister at a young age,
even before they could get engaged.

They were here and there doing revivals,
and depending on the Lord for their very survival.
After not very long, their first baby came,
and they had to really depend on Jesus' name.

There were times the money had gotten low,
but the call was still there, and Pastor D had to go.
Many, many souls have gotten saved,
and after many years, it still goes on today.

Souls Outreach continues to grow,
planted by Pastor Derrick, though he is getting old.
He will work till the Lord calls him in,
and yes, Sister Mavis, is still his best friend.

Children

God gave us children only on loan.
We are to train them, love them, and give them a home.

And when they are naughty and won't heed His word,
we need to keep trying, it needs to be heard.

Just think if someone had not prayed for you;
where would you be and what would you do?

So don't keep the knowledge all to yourself;
teach it to someone, don't put it on a shelf.

The wonderful word of God, we must share;
pass it on to someone, show them you care.

And then someday soon in church you'll be,
and there at the altar your child you'll see.

With arms uplifted and tears in their eyes,
surrendered to Jesus as they give Him their lives.

The angels in heaven rejoice when they see,
but not just the angels, my friend, you and me.

Africa

The aunties in Africa are wonderful cooks;
off the top of their heads, no need to use books.
All the wonderful curries, served up so nice,
with the beautiful roti, muffins, and rice.

When I visit Africa, it's easy to see,
I never go hungry, I just patiently
wait for the aunties, to finish the meat,
prepared in big pots with wood for the heat.

The bread they prepare while on the hot stone;
they stay there and tend it, don't leave it alone.
When you're in Africa, you'll always enjoy,
the foods from the fire, not a can from the store.

And when they come to your home in the USA for a visit,
it won't be the same as in Africa, will it?
But that is alright, for they will enjoy the foods
you'll prepare, which you bought from the store.

A Man's Gotta Do What A Man's Gotta Do

He cannot please everyone; God knows it's so true.
A man's gotta do what a man's gotta do!
Whenever you're thinking, "Why can't he please you,
especially when you've bitten off more than you can chew?"
And what to do next you have not a clue.
God made him the head, not me and not you.
Read it in the Bible, there is nothing new—
from beginning to end, every word is true.
That's why a man's gotta do what a man's gotta do!

Prophecy: Loryn and Merle

I feel in my spirit you're going to preach;
there are many souls God wants you to reach.

You've been in denial, you say, "No, not me,"
but think of your ministry and how the devil will flee.

You feel there are enough preachers right now in the world.
Yet there are so many men, women, boys, and girls,
who may not have heard the Word just yet.
And think of the blessings that you can get
by being obedient to our Lord.

So you and your wife get in one accord,
accept the call while you are young and strong.
The time is right now, don't wait too long,
because when you're old—don't get me wrong—
you can still preach and sing your song.
But it's best if you do it
while you're young and you're strong!

Leaders

Bless this house, dear Lord, I pray.
Keep this family strong every day.

Lead the head to make right decisions, I ask,
because to lead is never an easy task.

The leader must depend solely on You,
to reveal to him what he must do.

For you are the only one who won't make mistakes;
only You know the best way we should take.

You teach us each day to love and not hate;
if we don't love, hell is our fate.

Please, Lord, help us not to wait too late;
our deeds are recorded on a big slate.

And when the book is opened wide,
and You say, "Well done, please step inside."

To heaven then we will go to our rest,
and hear, "Dear pilgrim, you've done your best."

Thank You, Lord

With you in mind, our Jesus quietly
gave His life on a tree;
'twas a lonely place out on a hill—
a place called Calvary.

They stripped our Lord of His dignity.
They mocked Him till He died—
oh, can't you see?

His mom was there and at His feet she cried;
He was willing to die, never did deny.

The pain they inflicted on Him,
Mary's baby, heaven's gift,
gave His life out on a limb.

Now sometimes I cry when I stop
and think of all He has done;
I would be lost and without hope
and so would everyone.

Jesus paid the price that redeemed me
on that terrible day;
He paid a debt He did not owe,
and I owed a debt I could not pay

Thank God now I'm saved today.

Three Sisters

Three sisters lived on a hill
behind an iron gate.
They were all from the Fynn clan
with each other for a mate.

The older sister is Muriel,
with a quiet spirit is she;
sitting with a great big smile—
as content as could be.

The second sister is Peggy,
a lovely gift has she,
taking my measurements,
sewing me a dress to wear cross the sea.

The younger sister is Pamela Rose,
she takes care of the other two.
She does the cooking and cleaning,
doing all that she can do.

We were invited to visit them
and happy now we were
to sit and have a savory dish
and scones that will make you purr.

What hospitality we received
at the home of these lovely three.
I plan to go back there very soon,
just my friend Tersia and me!

Bunny Clothier

A soccer player named Bunny Clothier
from Kakamela he came.
He always played like a champ;
it must have been the name.

He did some schooling in a place
they call High Flats on a farm.
He married a lovely lady named Mary,
five children came along.
Pastor Clothier loves his family,
their bond is quite strong.

We'll all go to visit this great family
for a convention and some wonderful times.
We will try to see everything there;
it sounds like a lovely town.

And if we fall in love with Perth,
we may all just stick around.
I'm told they serve the Lord with a passion—
how wonderful that sounds.

Let's all get ready, dear friends, for the fun in 2013.
They said it will be the greatest convention
anyone has ever seen.

Phoenix

We visited a place called Phoenix
outside KwaZulu Natal.
Had a wonderful service
and Pastor Fynn preached quite well.

The Harvesters came with Lorne
and sang some wonderful songs.
I was so happy they invited me
with them to come along.

There were many beautiful people
at the church on that night.
Pastor D preached about hell, well,
it gave some quite a fright.

Frank came with the rest of us
and gave some more support.
We all went so anyone pregnant with sin
would surely want to abort.

I believe someone was saved and healed,
the Bible is very true.
The Word of God won't come back void,
not to me or to you.

Denise in Cape Town

You presented me with a book,
for the poems I write.
Just want to say thank you
and I love you with all my might.

Now it is true I have been blessed
with many friends around this world;
but you are one of the best I promise, my girl.

And should I close my eyes
and go to sleep before the next time,
where words will be sleeping
and there is no more rhyme.

I'll tell them in heaven to save you a seat,
you just be loving and helpful
to the next missionary auntie you meet.

Ruth Abrams

Your name in the Bible many times I have seen.
God long ago formed you to raise Meka Jean.

She is only a baby, so sweet and so fair.
The Lord sent her to Cape Town to live with you there.

If ever you wonder, *Why did this happen to me?*
Remember you're chosen, you're special, you see.

Paul is your cover; he will take care of you.
Please try to obey what he asks you to do.

I know he loves you; you are dear to his heart.
God put you together, so don't ever part.

You will be an example of what he wants you to be,
a good wife to Paul and a good friend to me.

Children in the Poor Camps

Why are you out here all alone?
Where are your parents? Are they at home?

You say you are hungry, when last did you eat?
Come, let us feed you; we have brought you a treat.

Jesus has sent us; He loves you so.
He wants us to tell you, He wants you to know.

Come have some food now, cooked just for you.
Go tell your parents there is food for them, too.

Squatter Camps in the Evening

We cooked up some food and took to the camp,
to feed little children; it's dark—bring a lamp.

But why are you outside alone in the dark?
They play in the trash pile; they don't have a park.

So happy to see us, they knew the black car.
They most all came running; they know who we are.

We tell them about Jesus, for He loves them so.
We share his love with them wherever we go.

There are some adults in the shadows they stand.
We offer them supper as we take their hand.

We invite them to visit the church where we go.
When asked will they come, they say they don't know.

Supper at Frankstown

Oh, what a supper we had at Frankstown;
Tersia made spareribs so nice, plump, and brown.

I thought of the poor ones who sleep under a tent;
with no food to eat, they don't have a cent.

Their children are hungry, the hunger pains growl;
please, Lord, do have mercy on each little child.

We know they would take anything we could spare;
so we go to the bridges and take food down there.

What can we do to help give them a start?
We tell them Jesus wants to come into their heart.

If they would just try him, then they can see,
what a great provider to them He will be.

Attention Please

Ladies and gentlemen, lassies and lads,
saints of the highest God,
I would like your attention and while I am speaking,
promise you will not nod.

You have a mission given by Jesus
and many have failed to do;
He did not just call me, my friends,
He has called all of you, too.

The things that I witnessed when last on a mission,
I promise you it's no lie.
If I had to live like many of those people,
well, I guess I would truly die.

No food, no clothes, no shoes on their feet,
no internal revenue.
You may be thinking you were not called
but I promise you were called, too.

Missionaries travel all over the world,
with sometime meager fare.
If when you here of a missionary traveling,
please give and help them get there.

The message of salvation—
people need to be saved—
needs preaching everywhere.
So please stop sitting with your arms and legs folded,
looking like you just don't care.

Join in and help us preach the gospel,
we need all of your help.
Some can give little and some can give much—
don't worry about just yourself.

You have loved ones who also need saving,
now tell me this, my friend;
if you just ignore and won't give a blessing,
what will God say in the end?

Johannesburg to Amsterdam

Multiple languages are what I have heard,
my trip going home on this big iron bird.

Amazing how it glides so smooth in the air,
with only our God to keep us up there.

Please, you are welcome, do just find your seat;
we will serve some refreshments and give you a treat.

And when you are tired you may take some naps;
but put on your seatbelt, lest turbulence haps.

Now we have landed but please keep your seat;
assistance is coming, my feet went to sleep.

I never did worry, I did say a prayer—
that Jesus our Savior would help us get there.

From Africa

Flying high above the clouds so white and billowy,
going so fast,
I can just gasp at the at sites that we can see.

Can't see the ground, can only hear the sound
of the plane on which I ride.
The sun is shining, it's a beautiful day—
so great to be alive.

What will I do with this gift of life God has given me?
Will I share freely with the others as God has set me free?
Will I obey His word ever faithful
and willingly step up to the challenge to give to the needy?
It's my responsibility,
over and over, we have heard the story,
of how our Savior died—He gave His life freely.

I cannot repay Him, not even if I tried;
I'll do my best to serve Him through others—
live a life that's sanctified, to be an example
so others may know Him,
which sometimes is a struggle—
but God knows I will try.

Community of Caring

A place is provided for the poor and the needy,
it's called COC.
They come in all sizes, all ages, all colors,
no prejudice there be.

It's Mother Kennedy whom God has chosen
along with her family,
to begin this work and take on the challenge here at COC.

She won't have to worry when she goes to heaven,
the love she shares has been free.
She is mentor and trainer,
so the work will continue
through people like you and me.

Drums

I listened to the drums last night as I tried to sleep.
I tried everything last night including counting sheep.
But after trying oh so hard, I finally gave up and said,
"Lord, won't you make them sleepy, so they will go to bed."

The Insulin

Please don't freeze this, it's very important—
a fact I tried to stress.
But there is a problem when there's no understanding
and yourself you fail to express.

They put my insulin into the freezer
and next morning it was froze.
Could not get upset because although I told them,
they really didn't know.

Well, I threw it away because it was ruined
and that was very bad.
Now to be without medicine so far from home,
is scary nevertheless.
God was with me and He always provided,
It was just another test.

Homeless

See them laying under the cardboard,
trying to get some sleep.

It's best to do it early night rather than late.
There are some people, who are naughty
and really up to no good.
They abuse and misuse the poor homeless person,
chasing them from their neighborhood.

Lord, will You please have mercy on
the least, the poor, and the lost.
I believe if they could change,
most would—change at any cost.

Those who have so much to share,
yet refuse to help those in need;
they don't realize it could be them—
with no shelter or food to eat.

Well, the day is coming and we don't know when,
we all will stand before Your throne.
The great book will be opened and we will all answer
for the deeds that we have done.

Some don't believe but they will find out
what the Bible says is real.
They are having fun now,
but on Judgment Day, I wonder how they will feel?

Wedding Promise

For the rest of our lives, we promise to love,
we want to be close as a hand in a glove.

We have found our true soulmate, though it did take time,
now I am yours and I'm glad you are mine.

We want to grow old together
and see the door close behind the last baby.

They will go to college or wherever they choose,
after eighteen we have paid our dues.

But up until then we are happy to be,
me loving you and you loving me.

Love is an action word; it's easy to do,
especially, my darling, when the love is so true.

We will stick close together like good superglue,
and if we get angry, we may throw a shoe.

But we promise from now on to love faithfully,
to share all we have, my dear, you and me.

Angels

You will send a legion if I'm in need,
to rescue me from Satan's deeds.

It is his plan to abort the test,
even though I try to do my best.

He does not know my best You require,
and my best for You I desire.

And as long as You will let me live,
my best for You I'll always give.

So some day when my life is done,
and I must face the setting sun,
I'll close my eyes, draw my last breath,
and surrender then to an ice-cold death.

Then I will see Your great big smile,
and hear You say, "Welcome home, my child."

My Dear Son

The child was naughty, I know it's true.
That's why I must depend on You,
to keep protection all around—
until the day of salvation is found.

By him the one I pray for much,
if You don't keep him with Your touch.
Satan will squeeze him in his clutch,
he will be lost and there he will be
in hell for all eternity.

You know I love him with all my heart,
before his breath could ever start.
You gave him life, now this I plead
that you, my Lord, will fill his need—
this son of mine who is my seed.

His life You're holding in Your hand.
It is a part of Satan's plan,
to just destroy him, but I know,
You promised he'd to heaven go.

And not just him but all of them,
these children you have given me.

Yes, my Lord, from my heart I plead—
You and I should never part.

Please help them to realize who You are,
before they stray out there too far.
You gave your life out on a tree,
not just for them but for them and for me.

It is Not Who You Are

The older you get, the deeper it goes,
that spirit which destroyed your manhood.

It knows the path to take,
slithers through you like a snake.

All those gestures that you make,
you know they are not real—they are fake.

You were not born a girl, you are confused,
the many people from who you were abused.

For the filth you know you did not choose.
God have mercy on the boys,
the enemy that plays them like toys,
then watches as their boyhood fades,
as they wither and die with the dreaded AIDS.

Oh, my God, won't you help these
who all too often have heard please
from messengers both far and near.

We bring the Word for them to hear
so that they won't act so strange
and in their hearts will want to change.

And change they must before it's too late,
when all too soon they'll have a date
with death for that will be their fate.

Oh, please don't let it be said, "Too late."

A Plea for Help

A homosexual is what they say,
as if I want to stay this way.
They just don't know how hard I've tried
to lose these sins to which I'm tied.

I pray often to the Lord, "Please
help me lose the ties like these.
We're so bound but not our fault;
we were most raped and during onslaught,
the sins came in and took us over,
when we were young and had no cover."

"Where was my mother when first I was touched?
I really needed her very much.
If she had just walked in and she could see,
what this man had done to me."

"Lord, please hear me when I pray.
I don't want to stay this way."

Obedient Spirit

"An obedient spirit," is what the Lord said to man,
"then you can eat the good of the land."

If we really love Him, this is what we will do.
We will seek to please Him and always be true.

There are many distractions in this world today,
but people don't want to live right or pray.

I have a message, friend, and to you I must say,
"Seek the Lord with all your heart,
and make the change today."

"If not, you will be sorry, for Satan has a plan;
if you fail to serve the Lord, Satan will destroy a man."

Betty

They say I am a poet;
I put the words to rhyme.
I did not know I could do it;
it took me a long, long time.

But now the gift comes naturally,
I can write about all kind.
I thank the Lord for He gave to me
the knowing how to rhyme.

www.ingramcontent.com/pod-product-compliance
Lightning Source LLC
Chambersburg PA
CBHW070810050426
42452CB00011B/1981